WHEN DID YOU DIE?

B. McCall Barbour

Copyright March 2013

Reprinted *with* Permission *from*
Theodore C. Danson Smith

CROWN
CHRISTIAN
PUBLICATIONS
Royal Reading

FAITHfortheFAMILY.com

WHEN DID YOU DIE?
& HOW TO DIE DAILY

Reprinted with permission from Theodore C. Danson Smith
& B. McCall Barbour Publishing • Copyright © 2013
All Scripture quotation are taken from the Authorized King James Version
Crown Christian Publications
Powell, Tennessee · 37849
CrownChristianPublications.com
FAITH*for the*FAMILY.com

ISBN: 978-1-58981-660-2

Design & layout by Ryan Keiter

Printed in the United States of America

WHEN DID YOU DIE?

B. McCall Barbour

Copyright March 2013

Reprinted *with* Permission *from*
Theodore C. Danson Smith

CROWN
CHRISTIAN
PUBLICATIONS
Royal Reading

FAITH*for the*FAMILY.com

"Except a corn of wheat fall into the ground and die, it abideth alone: but if it die, it bringeth forth much fruit"

John 12:24

Contents

Preface

In my possession I have a marked copy of the little book that Lee Roberson said changed his life.

While visiting the B. McCall Barbour bookstore in Edinburgh, Scotland the owner asked me if I knew Lee Roberson. Of course, I was happy to talk to Mr. Danson Smith about Dr. Roberson and to tell him of my personal acquaintance and friendship with him.

After a while the dear man said to me, "The book that changed Dr. Roberson's life came from this bookstore." I knew the story that was being told because I had heard it years before from Dr. Roberson.

When I asked the owner for additional copies of that book I learned it had been out of print for more than 30 years and that I was the first to ask for a copy in many years.

My friend, you have in your hand that book and a companion of that book from a series by B. McCall Barbour on, "Death to Self." May this be as life-changing for you as it was for Dr. Lee Roberson and for me.

Clarence Sexton
Acts 5:42

Tribute to Dr. Lee Roberson
written by Dr. J. R. Faulkner

June 8, 1914–June 10, 2009

Lee Edward Roberson (24 November 1909–29 April 2007) was the pastor of Highland Park Baptist Church and the founder of Tennessee Temple University in Chattanooga, Tennessee, and Camp Joy in Harrison, Tennessee.

He was born in a two-room log cabin on November 24, 1909, and spent his first two years on a farm near English, Indiana, a small town in the southern part of the state. In 1911, his parents, Mr. and Mrs. Charles E. Roberson, took him to a farm near Louisville, Kentucky, where his father farmed, worked on streetcars, and built homes to make a living. At the age of 14, he was led to the Lord by his faithful Sunday School teacher, Mrs. Daisy Hawes, and joined the Cedar Creek Baptist Church outside of Louisville.

After spending two years at the Louisville Male High School, where he received a diploma in public accounting when he was 14 years old, Dr. Roberson then attended the Fern Creek High School and graduated after four years. While a student, he played football with the high school team.

Dr. Roberson entered Old Bethel College in Russellville, Kentucky, in 1926, and finished the first year. There he worked at various jobs from washing dishes to scrubbing floors to pay his way. From Old Bethel College, he went to the University of Louisville to complete his college work with a major in history. He also completed his work for a degree at the Southern Baptist Theological Seminary in Louisville. At the age of 19, he was called to a church in Jeffersontown, Kentucky, which he did not accept.

In his early years, Dr. Roberson was well known as a singer. Having studied at the Cincinnati Conservatory of Music and with the well-known teacher, John Samples, of Chicago, his services as a vocalist were in great demand. He served as a soloist on the staff of radio station WHAS of Louisville, Kentucky, and WSM out of Nashville. Doors were opening in the field of secular music. Dr. Roberson could have signed a contract with a certain man in the city of Nashville that, no doubt, would have led him to the top in music. However, he felt that this was not the thing the Lord wanted for him; so he refused to sign the contract.

The first church that Dr. Roberson served as pastor was in Germantown, Tennessee, while he was going to college. In 1932, he was called to be pastor of the Temple Baptist Church in Green Brier, Tennessee. It was there that he discovered the truth of the second coming of Christ. After three years with the Green Brier Church, where the Lord wonderfully blessed, Dr. Roberson entered full-time evangelistic work in 1935. He served as evangelist of the Birmingham Baptist Association, and within two years, he conducted some fifty revivals in the Birmingham area.

It was while he was in Birmingham that he met Miss Caroline Allen, who, on October 9, 1937, became Mrs. Lee Roberson.

On the first Sunday in November 1937, Dr. Roberson became pastor of the First Baptist Church in Fairfield, Alabama.

In 1939, Brother Roberson was asked to be the state evangelist for Alabama. He felt this was not the Lord's will for him at the time, so the offer was not accepted. On May 2, 1941, Lee Anne, the Roberson's oldest child, was born.

After five years with the Fairfield church, Dr. Roberson was called to the Highland Park Baptist Church in Chattanooga, in November of 1942. Dr. Roberson, our pastor, was a man of God at home as well as at church. He set an example of faithfulness and devotion to his family and to his convictions before his church and to the entire world. At home, he sought to teach his children in the fear and admonition of the Lord around a daily family altar, which reflected itself in the lives of the children.

Dr. Roberson's devotion to duty and to his convictions laid upon him a demanding schedule that caused him, throughout his life, to get up early and to burn the midnight oil in prayer and study of the Word of God and the writings of others that he might maintain his burden to reach as many souls for Christ as he could, by every possible means. New sermons were constantly pouring from his soul and new books from his pen.

Whether he was speaking from the pulpit of the Highland Park Baptist Church, the chapel platform of Tennessee Temple

Schools, to his Men's Bible Class, or at one of many other special services, his messages were always fresh, fervent, and filled with the power of God. In speaking of him, someone said, "He is truly the Spurgeon of our times."

Dr. Roberson's daily schedule began with Bible study and prayer at 6:30 in the morning, followed by breakfast and devotions with his family, a broadcast beginning at 8:30 a.m., and a chapel service at Tennessee Temple Schools at 10:00. His morning hours were also filled with private conferences with church people and students of Tennessee Temple Schools. His daily visitation program took him into the numerous hospitals of the city as well as homes of the church members.

He preached his last service as pastor of Highland Park Baptist Church on April 27, 1983, but continued in the work of the Lord. Dr. Roberson preached across the nation and also published many books. He continued to serve until his death.

Lee Roberson died two years after his wife's death. His legacy includes strong preaching, Bible based standards, and an uncompromising devotion to God.

Dr. J.R. Faulker
Lee Roberson's "Armour Bearer"

Faithful associate pastor to Lee Roberson, 40 years

Book 1

WHEN DID YOU DIE?

A *strange* question? True! Arresting? Yes! Absurd? No! Sensible? Quite! Searching? Surely! Impertinent? No! Important? Yes, supremely so! It is of the most vital and immediate importance for every child of God. Listen to the simple statements of God's Word:- "Ye *are* dead" (Colossians 3:3); "We that are dead" (Romans 6:2); "*Crucified* with Him" (Romans 6: 6); "I *am crucified* with Christ" (Galatians 2:20); " We *being* dead" (I Peter 2:24) ; "Except a corn of wheat fall into the ground and *die*, it abideth alone: but if it *die*, it bringeth forth much fruit" (John 12:24).

To ask the question by no means implies that pharisaical attitude of spiritual pride indicated by the words:- "certain which trusted in themselves that they were righteous, and despised others" (Luke 18:9). The question is asked with sincere and loving concern for all of God's dear children everywhere. May this great fact of our "so great salvation" (Hebrews 2:3)- "ye *are* dead" be frankly and fully faced by all. This will be for our own greatest spiritual good, for untold blessing to others, and for the glorifying of "the great God and our Saviour Jesus Christ" (Titus 2:13).

Let not, then, the question be treated with indifference, either because it *seems* "too doctrinal," "too deep," or "too dry." To treat it so is to do an injustice to the Love of God; to bring about a loss to our eternal welfare; and to give infinite delight to the arch-deceiver of our souls.

There need be no fear in frankly facing this question. If it is frankly faced we shall know the doctrine that it is of God (John 7:17). The Holy Spirit, as we obey Him, will guide us into all truth (John 16:13). The truth shall no longer be "too deep" or "too dry," but shall become to us a "delight" as it works for our deliverance. We shall get to know it as "the truth shall make you free" (John 8:32).

When did *you* "Die"? The answer, simply stated, is-"*When Jesus died.*" This, of course, is as viewed from God's standpoint. In His reckoning "It is finished." But-ah, but, alas on our side, and in the experience of many,-shall we say of the mass,-of God's dear children this "dying" has never yet taken place. We are slow to apprehend, and to appreciate the meaning of this truth, and to appropriate the fullness of God's salvation which is in Christ Jesus. The "fullness" of that salvation saves us not only from our sin and from our sinning, but-note this-from that greatest of all enemies, *ourselves*. In God's plan and purpose, and through His divine provision, *we must die*, or remain unfruitful. Let this be emphasized by repetition of the very words of Jesus Himself: "Except a corn of wheat fall unto the ground and die, it abideth alone; but if it die, it bringeth forth much fruit" (John 12:24).

Happy indeed are they who know, in their experience, the blessedness of being "born again" (John 3:3), and so possessing Jesus Christ as their substitutionary Saviour from their sinful past. But, indeed, *thrice blessed* are they who have "followed on to know" the death of *self*, through their identification with Him on the cross,–who have been "crucified with Christ" (Galatians 2:20),–who have *died* with Him (Romans 6:3)–have been "buried with Him" (Romans 6:4),–have risen with Him "in newness of life" (Romans 6:4), and who are now "dead indeed unto sin, but alive unto God" (Romans 6:11). Dear friend, is this your experience? We affectionately ask, "When did *you die* ?"

> "On the cross of Calvary
> Jesus died for you and me;
> There He shed His precious blood
> That from sin we might be free.
> There was full atonement made,
> There my heavy debt was paid.
> It was for me that Jesus died
> On the cross of Calvary."

Yes, this is blessedly true; "It was for me that Jesus died." But there also "I," "Self," "the flesh," *was crucified with Him*. There "I" *died* with Him. As Paul has said, –"I am crucified with Christ: nevertheless I live; yet not I, but Christ liveth in me: and the life which I now live in the flesh I live by the faith of the Son of God, who loved me, and gave himself for me." (Galatians 2:20)

> "It is most important for us to understand what are the characteristics of the *self-life*, and how impossible it is, when under its sway, to live a spiritual life, and wield spiritual weapons in the service of God. It is useless exhorting the 'flesh' to be 'spiritual'; and yet the flesh, seeking to live a 'spiritual' life, and calling itself 'spiritual,' is the meaning of the discrepancy in so many Christian lives of today. We get light in our minds, spiritual phrases on our tongues, call our 'work' spiritual,—whilst we ourselves live after the flesh in greater or lesser degree all the time."
>
> (J. Penn-Lewis)

What, then, let us ask, is this "I," this "Self" that must *die*,—that must be "crucified with Christ"? The following summary of its characteristics will help to make this plain:—

SELF

"The last enemy destroyed in the believer is *Self*. It dies hard. It will make any concessions if allowed to live. Self will permit the believer to do anything, give anything, sacrifice anything, suffer anything, be anything, go anywhere, take any liberties, bear any crosses, afflict soul or body to any degree-anything if it can only hold sway.

It will allow victory over pride, penuriousness and passion, if not destroyed itself. It will permit any number of rivals so long as it can be promised the first place. It will consent to live in a hovel, in a garret, in the slums, in far-away heathendom, if only its life can be spared. It will endure any garb, any fare, any menial service rather than surrender.

But this concession must not be granted. *Self* is too great a foe to the child of God. It is everywhere present. It is the fly that spoils the ointment, the little fox that spoils the vine. It provokes God and man and its own possessor. It drives to insomnia, invalidism and insanity. It produces disorder and derangement in the whole physical, mental, moral and spiritual constitution. It talks back, excuses and vindicates itself, and never apologizes. It must *die*.

'Dying to self' is a poetic expression. It sounds romantic, heroic, chivalrous, supernatural, saintlike. It is beautiful to read about, fascinating to write about, refreshing to dream about. But it is hard to do. But it must be done. There is no abiding peace, power or prosperity without it.

We must *die* to good deeds and to bad deeds, to successes and to failures, to superiority and to inferiority, to leading and to following, to exaltation and to humiliation, to our life work, to our friends, to our foes, to every manifestation of *self* and to *self* itself. Jesus said, 'The hour is come that the Son of Man should be glorified. Except a corn of wheat fall into the ground and *die*, it abideth alone, but if it *die* it bringeth forth much fruit. He that loveth his life shall lose it, but he that loseth his life (himself) shall find it.' 'He that will come after Me, let him deny himself.' Christ could not be glorified till after death, nor can He be glorified in His people till *self dies*. In close connection with this passage Jesus says, 'I, if I be lifted up from the earth, will draw all men unto Me' (John 12:32). Self lifted up repels. Lifted up with Christ on the cross it draws. Happy those who can say with Paul, from a real experience, 'I am crucified with Christ: nevertheless I live; yet not I, but Christ liveth in me' (Galatians 2: 20)."

(W. J. Mosier)

With satanic subtlety we are deceived by *self*. "Even our sacrifices and self-denials may be selfish," says Dr. A. B. Simpson. "Yes, our satisfaction may be selfish. Self can get up and pray, and sit down and say: 'What a lovely prayer!' Self can preach a sermon and save souls and go home, pat itself on the back and say, or let the devil say it through him: 'You did it splendidly; what a useful man you are!' Self can be burned to death and be proud of its fortitude. Yes, we can have religious selfishness as well as carnal selfishness."

"There is a foe whose hidden power
     The Christian well may fear,
More subtle far than inbred sin,
     And to the heart more dear.

It is the power of *selfishness*,
     It is the willful 'I,'
And ere my Lord can live in me
     My very *self* must *die*."

Aptly has it been called "This cruel *self*." It is. And no doubt, in deepest earnestness, many a true believer prays:–

"My Saviour, Thou hast offered rest,
     Oh! give it then to me;
The rest of ceasing from myself,
     To find my all in Thee.
This cruel self! Oh, how it strives
     And works within my breast,
To come between Thee and my soul,
     And keeps me back from rest."

Reader, has this been *your* prayer? Then, my friend, you need *pray it no longer*. Begin to *appropriate*, at this moment, what Christ now offers to you. *Ask* no more, but *take* what now He proffers—deliverance from "this cruel *self.*" Comply with His conditions. Identify yourself with Him upon the cross. Be "crucified with Christ." Experimentally "*die.*" Find your deliverance from, and victory over, *self*, through death. Possess your longed-for and prayed-for *rest*,—the rest of "ceasing from yourself."

Be not deceived! Do not endeavour to *crucify yourself.* Accept, by faith, the fact that God has already crucified you. "Ye *are* dead." We are not called to a process of *self crucifixion*, but to the acceptance of a *crucifixion of self* already accomplished. Ye "*have been* crucified." By an instantaneous death we have an instantaneous deliverance, to be worked out in experience. Man's method is a gradual crucifixion of *self*, and consequently a continual slavery. Too frequently we are deceived into the crucifying of "things," and "habits," and "desires," and "inclinations," and "affections," in a piece-meal fashion. God's method is drastic and decisive. *Self has been* crucified with Christ in one act. Henceforth "ye *are* dead." "They that are Christ's *have crucified* the flesh with the affections and lusts. If we live in the Spirit, let us also walk in the Spirit" (Galatians 5:24, 25).

Now then, the love of Christ overmasters us, the conclusion at which we have arrived being this—that One having died for all, *His death was their death*, and that He died for all, in order that the living may *no longer live unto themselves*, but to Him Who died for them and rose again (II Corinthians 5:14, 15).

"A clergyman once said, 'Do you know that Campbell Morgan came to this country, and preached one sermon that destroyed forty years of my sermons? Forty years I had been preaching on the duty of sacrifice—denying things to ourselves, giving up this and that. We practiced it in our family. We would give up butter one week, and try to use the money in some way that God would bless. Another week we would give up something else. And so on. Campbell Morgan said that what we needed to give up was not *things* but *self*. And that was the only thing we had not given up in our home. We had given up everything under the sun but *self*.' " (S.S. Times)

Beloved, have you seen the vision of yourself, crucified upon the cross in the person of Jesus Christ? If not, get aside with God. In the stillness of His presence let Him speak to you.

> "I am crucified with Jesus,
> And the cross has set me free;
> I have risen again with Jesus,
> And He lives and reigns in me.
>
> It is sweet to *die* with Jesus,
> To the world, and *self*, and sin
> It is sweet to live with Jesus,
> As He lives and reigns within.
>
> This the story of the Master,
> Through the Cross, He reached the Throne,
> And, like Him, our path to glory
> Ever leads through death alone."

"Follow *me*!"

Thus it is that we may say: "the law of the Spirit of life in Christ Jesus hath made me free from the law of sin and death" (Romans 8:2).

But, again we warn-be not deceived! This is no doctrine of "sinless perfection," nor is it of "annihilation of the old nature," nor is it "suppression" and ceaseless striving to keep under "the flesh." It simply is *appropriation* of the person of Jesus Christ Himself as our very life, and a henceforth reckoning ourselves to be dead indeed unto sin, and a yielding of ourselves unto Him as those who are alive from the dead (Romans 6:13). Insomuch as we let Him live, by so much shall the Christian life be truly lived in us, for Christ, not I, is the life.

"Likewise *reckon* ye also yourselves *to be dead* indeed unto sin, but *alive unto God* through Jesus Christ our Lord.

Let not sin therefore reign in your mortal body, that ye should obey it in the lusts thereof.

Neither yield ye your members as instruments of unrighteousness unto sin: but yield yourselves unto God, as those that are *alive from the dead*, and your members as instruments of righteousness unto God" (Romans 6:11-13).

"If ye then be risen with Christ, seek those things which are above, where Christ sitteth on the right hand of God.

Set your affection on things above, not on things on the earth.

For ye are dead, and your life is hid with Christ in God.

When *Christ, who is our life*, shall appear, then shall ye also appear with him in glory.

Mortify (make dead) therefore your members which are upon the earth" (Colossians 3:1-5).

"But put ye on the Lord Jesus Christ, and make not provision for the flesh, to fulfil the lusts thereof" (Romans 13:14). (Dead men need no attention.)

RECKON

"There's a little word that the Lord has given,
For our help in the hour of need-
Let us *reckon* ourselves to be dead to sin,
To be dead to sin indeed.

There's another word that the Lord has given,
In the very same verse we read:-
Let us *reckon* ourselves as alive in Him,
As alive and alive indeed.

Let us *Reckon! Reckon! Reckon!*
Reckon rather than feel!
Let us be true to the reckoning,
And God will make it real."

(Dr. A. B. Simpson)

How "Reckoning" Works

"It is said that many centuries ago, a young man came to a godly saint, and asked what this meant: *What is it to be dead?* The old saint told him to go to the grave of Brother Thomas, who had recently died, and call him all the vile, contemptuous names he could think of,-to abuse him in every way, -and see what Brother Thomas would reply.

So the young man went out to the grave, and poured forth a terrible tirade against the departed one. Then he stopped and listened, and, after a little, returned to the house. The old saint asked him if he had done as instructed, and he answered, 'Yes.' 'Then what did brother Thomas reply?' 'Nothing.'

Then the young man was told to go back and speak of all the good things he could think of about Brother Thomas, to flatter him, and praise him to the skies in every possible way. So the young man went back and poured forth a glowing tribute to the departed one, then listened for the answer. But none came.

Upon his return he was again asked, 'What did brother Thomas reply?' 'Nothing.' 'Then,' the old saint said, 'That is what it means to be dead.' It is not to be moved, either by what is said against us, or by praises that are given us. Are you 'dead'?"

Beloved, is this your experience?

"I've reckoned myself to be dead unto sin,
And risen with Christ, and now He lives within;
The 'life more abundant' He gives unto me,
This overflow life gives me full victory."

"The life *which I now live* in the flesh" (body) (Galatians 2:20). Well, what life is that? Is it "Not I, but Christ?"

"For even hereunto were ye called: because Christ also suffereth for us, leaving us an example, that ye should follow His steps:

Who did no sin, neither was guile found in His mouth:

Who, when he was reviled, reviled not again; when he suffered, he threatened not; but committed himself to him that judgeth righteously:

Who his own self bare our sins in his own body on the tree, that we, *being dead to sins*, should live unto righteousness: by whose stripes ye were healed" (I Peter 2:21-24).

"He died for all, that they which live *should not henceforth live unto themselves*, but unto him which died for them, and rose again" (II Corinthians 5:15).

"Our old man is crucified with him, that the body of sin might be destroyed, that *henceforth we should not serve sin*. For he that *is dead* is freed from sin" (Romans 6:6, 7).

This blessed attitude is ensured, maintained, and experienced as we reckon ourselves as "alive unto God," and so yield ourselves, and all our members, unto Him.

> "I've yielded to God, and I'm saved every hour,
> I've yielded to God, and I feel His sweet power.
> I've trusted His promises, not one has failed
> Of all His good Word, tho' the tempter assailed.
> Sweet, quiet, yielded life,
> Blessed rest from all storm and strife;
> God's own peace now fills my soul,
> As on Him my way I roll."

"*If it die*, it bringeth forth much fruit." The life is fruitful, fertile, fragrant, full and free. This is not only "life," but "life more abundant." "Fruit" is what glorifies God. "Fruit" is the sure proof of discipleship.

"Herein is my Father glorified, that ye bear much fruit; so shall ye be my disciples" (John 15:8). The only "fruit" that pleases God, and that can glorify Him, is "the fruit of the Spirit." "The fruit of the Spirit is love, joy, peace, longsuffering, gentleness, goodness, faith, meekness, temperance (self-control): against such there is no law" (Galatians 5:22-23). Such "fruit" can come from only one root—no other than the Holy Spirit. The "fruit" that is the outcome of "the flesh," no matter how beautiful it may appear, is ever and only "absolute corruption."

"Absolute honesty," "absolute purity," "absolute love," "absolute selflessness," —these are found in *Christ* alone. All "holiness" that we can ever have is found in *Him*. "But of him are ye in Christ Jesus, who of God is made unto us wisdom, and righteousness, and sanctification (i.e., holiness), and redemption: that, according as it is written, He that glorieth, let him glory in the Lord" (I Corinthians 1:30, 31}.

> "This the secret of the holy,
>   Not our holiness, but *Him*:
> Jesus! empty us and fill us
>   With Thy fulness to the brim."

"I know that in me, (that is, in my flesh,) dwelleth no good thing" (Romans 7:18). Well did Paul know this fact. Nevertheless, he has made it plain, that it is just *in these mortal bodies* that the life of Jesus is to be manifested and magnified. "Always bearing about in the body the dying of the Lord Jesus, that the life also of Jesus might be made manifest in our body. For we which live are alway delivered unto death for Jesus' sake, that the life also of Jesus might be made manifest in our mortal flesh" (II Corinthians 4:10, 11).

Thus, in whatsoever sphere, however lowly or exalted, and with whatsoever talents—many or few—we may have been gifted, there, and by such means, as we "let the beauty of Jesus be seen in us," will others be attracted by Him. He it is Who is the drawing power. It is not us. We are ever the privileged "channels." "Channels,"—but, let it never be forgotten, "channels *only.*" Is there anything more blessed than to be such a channel? Is there anything more difficult to "the flesh" than to be a "channel *only*"? Just "a channel "—*Christ* "the power." Just "a branch"—*Christ* "the vine." Just "a vessel"—*Christ* "the treasure." Just "a lamp"—*Christ* "the light." Just "a cup"—*Christ* "the water."

When we are satisfied to just be such—then, and only then, with "all His wondrous power flowing through us, He will use us, every day and every hour." It was for this holy and exalted service of witnessing for Him, that He purchased us with "his own blood" (Acts 20:28). And it is by our identification with Him in His death and resurrection, that we shall find we are made vessels "meet for the Master's use" (II Timothy 2:21).

Let it, then, be recognized and acknowledged that "ye are not your own, for ye are bought with a price," and, let the injunction be heeded,— "therefore glorify God in your body, and in your spirit, which are God's" (I Corinthians 6:19, 20)

> "Witnessing Thy power to save me,
>   Setting free from *self* and sin;
> Thou Who bought'st me to possess me,
>   In Thy fulness, Lord, come in."

"*We also* should walk in newness of life" (Romans 6:4).

> "Buried with Christ, and raised with Him, too;
> What is there left for me to do?
> Simply to cease from struggling and strife,
> Simply to 'walk in newness of life.' "

"As ye have therefore received Christ Jesus the Lord, so *walk* ye in Him" (Colossians 2:6).

"He that saith he abideth in him ought himself also so to *walk*, even as he walked" (I John 2:6).

"For even hereunto were ye called: because Christ also suffered for us, leaving us an example, that *ye should follow his steps*' (I Peter 2:21).

Who is sufficient for these things? "Faithful is He that calleth you, Who also will do it" (I Thessalonians 5:24).

"I will dwell in them, and *walk* in them" (II Corinthians 6:16). Reckon on *Him*! Appropriate *Him*! Let *Him*!

Thus "indwelt," the life shall be "Not I, but Christ."

> "Not merely in the words you say,
> Not merely in your deeds confessed,
> But in the most unconscious way
> Is Christ expressed.

Is it a beatific smile?
A holy light upon your brow?
Oh, no; I felt His presence when
You laughed just now!

For me, 'twas not the truth you taught,
To you so clear, to me so dim;
But when you came to me you brought
A sense of *Him*!

And from your eyes He beckons me;
And from your heart His love is shed;
Till I lose sight of you,—and see
The *Christ* instead."

(Anonymous)

"Not I, but Christ, be honoured, loved, exalted;
Not I, but Christ, be seen, be known, be heard;
Not I, but Christ, in every look and action,
Not I, but Christ, in every thought and word."

If we would "know Him" in "the power of His
resurrection," we must be identified with Him,—
according to our measure,—in "the fellowship of His

sufferings," and be "made conformable unto His death" (dying as He died). (Philippians 3:10.)

"If any man serve me, let him follow me; and where I am, there shall also my servant be: if any man serve me, him will my Father honour" (John 12:26).

> "Dying with Jesus, by death reckoned mine
> Living with Jesus a new life Divine;
> Looking to Jesus till glory doth shine‑
> Moment by moment, O Lord, I am Thine."

> "How may I know the victory?
>   So many cry;
> Commit *thyself* to Calvary
>   Consent to *die*.

> God's way of gain is seeming loss;
>   We *die* to live;
> And His life comes, as to the cross
>   My life I give."
>   (H.E.J.)

"If we will acquire the habit of saying 'No!' not only to our bad, but to our good self; if we will daily deliver ourselves up to death for Jesus' sake; if we will take up our cross and follow the Master, though it be to His grave, we will become increasingly conscious of being possessed by a richer, deeper, Diviner life than our own."

(Dr. F. B. Meyer)

When we have thus "*Died*," we shall no longer seek to gratify ourselves by giving a "piece of our mind" (or may it not more often be a piece of our "tongue"), to those whose behavior we think warrants it, or whom we think deserve it. "Bitterness," "wrath," "anger" and "clamour" will be put away. Husbands will not be "bitter" against their wives. Wives will not indulge in "railing" at their husbands. Words with a cruel, cutting sting in them, will not be sent forth, to rankle in the bosom of another. And they will not need to be so sorrowfully and shamefully atoned for and withdrawn.

Nor, when we have thus "*Died*," shall we seek to "be" other than our true, natural selves. The "artificial,"-the "unreal,"-will go,-with all "affectation."

Perhaps amongst the readers of this little message there may happen to be some "servant of Jesus Christ," some minister of the Gospel, whom God is not using just as frequently and as abundantly as He might. Can the reason be, my brother, that the "dying" has not yet taken place, and that the sermons preached have a subtle something lurking in them, calculated to bring gratification to "Self," rather than glory to God and good to the souls of men?

In the *Life of F. B. Meyer,* his biographer tells how that, after he became assistant to the Rev. C. M. Birrell at Liverpool he fell so completely under the spell of that great and notable preacher's "polished, classic style," that he "soon became Birrellised"; that, as the younger man, he "followed the older, gaining indeed concentration and style in the process, but getting into bondage from which afterwards he was only delivered by a great spiritual crisis.

"But"-the record at the early period of his life goes on,-and oh, the pathos of that "but"-"there was only a scanty record of conversions, and, though he became popular, he scarcely imagined himself to be successful as a minister of Jesus Christ.

In this condition he met D. L. Moody, beneath whose "rugged utterance" he recognized "a spiritual power which he himself longed to possess." It was from Moody "that he learnt the art of winning men and women for Christ." And "perhaps the chief lesson Moody taught the young pastor was, that to do good work in the world he must be *himself.*"

And is not the shortest, surest way of becoming one's true natural *self*, to be found in bringing that same "self" to the place of "death." Later on, herein, Dr. Meyer tells, in his own language, of the great moment when "self" was, by his own act and will, placed on the cross,—an act which, surely, became the gateway to such an extraordinary life of fruit-bearing and usefulness as so truly became his.

WHEN THEY DIED

It is instructive and encouraging to know how others, who have "Died," have faced the crisis and come through to the blessedness of this "death-born-life that never dies."

Dr. A. B. Simpson writes concerning this "great transaction" in his own experience:

> "The death of Christ simply means for me that when He died, I died, and in God's view I am now as if I had been executed for my own sin, and am now recognised as another person who has risen with Christ, and is justified from his former sins because he has been executed for them, 'For he that is dead is freed from sin.'
>
> Not only so, it is the secret of my sanctification, for, on the cross of Calvary, I, the sinful self, was put to death; and when I lay myself over with Him upon that cross and reckon myself dead, Christ's risen life passes into me, and it is no longer my struggling, my goodness, or my badness, but my Lord Who lives in me, and through Whom, while I abide in Him, I am counted even as He, and enabled to walk even as He walked.

Beloved, have you entered into the death of
Christ and counted it yours, and, through it,
are you now alive unto Him in the power of
His resurrection?"

(From "The Christ Life")

The Rev. F. B. Meyer, D.D., relates, when he "*Died*"
with Jesus, as follows:-

"On the cross Jesus Christ offered a
substitutionary sacrifice for the sins of the
whole world...God sent His Son in the
likeness of sinful flesh and for sin. 'For sin' is
substitutionary. 'In the likeness of sinful flesh'
is the reference of the cross to sanctification.
On the cross God nailed, in the person of
Christ, the likeness of our sinful flesh. I cannot
explain it to you more than that; but I know
this-that next to seeing Jesus as my Sacrifice,
nothing has revolutionized my life like seeing
the effigy of my sinful *self* in the sinless, dying
Saviour. I say to myself...God has nailed the
likeness of my *self-life* to the cross. If, then,
God has treated the likeness of my sinful *self*,

when borne by the sinless Christ, as worthy of His curse, how terrible, in God's sight, it must be for myself to hug it, and embrace it, and live in it!

Christ and I are one. In Him I hung there. I came to an end of myself in Christ, and, kneeling at His cross, I took the position of union with Him in His death, and I consigned my *self-life* to the cross. It was as though I took my *self-life*, with its passions, its choices, its yearnings after perfection, its fickleness, its judgment of others, its uncharity—I took it as a felon and said: 'Thou art cursed, thou shalt die. My God nailed thee to that cross. Come, thou shalt come. I put thee there by my choice, by my will, by my faith. Hang there.'

After that moment, that decisive moment in my life, I have ever reckoned that myself is on the cross, and that the death of Christ lies between me and it...

Whilst the Spirit of God, in the depth of your heart crucifies the *self-life*, He makes Jesus Christ a living, bright reality. He fixes your thoughts upon Jesus. You do not think about the Spirit, you hardly think about the Spirit, you hardly think about *self*, but you think much about your Lord.

O man and woman, forgive me! It is a very broken, broken way of putting the deepest mystery of the Bible, but I can only ask that the Holy Spirit may make you know what it is to have Jesus as the center and origin of your life. The fountain and origin, hitherto, has been *self*, has it not? Oh, cursed *self*! Barabbas, Barabbas, to the cross! The world says: 'Not Christ, but Barabbas-*self*.' The Christian says: 'Not Barabbas, but Christ.' May God explain this to you for His Name's sake!"

Of Dr. C. I. Scofield his biographer, C. G. Trumbull, writes:-

> "The secret of Dr. Scofield's 'Victorious Life' is the same and only secret of the Victorious Life of every believer, wherever such victory is experienced:-he 'let go, and he let God.' He did not try to add his efforts to God's finished and perfect work. He yielded and believed; and the Captain of his Salvation, instantly making him more than conqueror, led him in triumph...Although, as a pastor in Dallas for several years, God had greatly blessed him in his own life,-and in his studies in the Word, to himself and to others,-he had not yet entered into the New Testament teaching of the life of power and victory.

> ...The light broke in through a study of the threefold experience of the Apostle Paul. Beginning as a *self-satisfied*, *self-righteous* legalist, Paul met Jesus on the Damascus-road and became a justified man; but still a man under the defeats recorded in the seventh of

Romans. Passing, then, into the marvelous victories of the eighth of Romans, it was plain that Paul ascribed these victories (Romans 8:2) to the new life in Christ Jesus, as energized and made effectual through the indwelling Holy Spirit. The eager seeker found that great chapter athrill with the Spirit. Passing over the parenthetic ninth, tenth, and eleventh chapters, to the twelfth—the true continuation of the eighth—he found the disclosure of the step into victory—and not victory over the Adamic *self* merely, *but into the whole life of fruitful service and fullness of joy.* The new act of faith demanded the presentation (or yielding) of the body; demanded not only the cessation of conscious resistance to Christ, but also the acceptance of the Christ-life plan as one of sacrifice. A life no longer to serve *self* but Christ. The thing demanded was an act, as definite as the act of faith in which the new life began.

When this was perceived, the answer in Scofield's soul was 'Obedience.' *From that*

moment a new experience of fruitful service and
of inner blessing began."

"To one who asked George Müller the secret of his
service, he replied:-

There was a day when I *died*; and, as he spoke, he bent
lower, until he almost touched the floor. Continuing,
he added, 'Died to George Müller, his opinions,
preferences, tastes, and will; died to the world, its
approval or censure; died to the approval or blame even
of my brethren or friends; and since then I have studied
only to show myself approved unto God.'"

Age is no limit to this experience of "Christ the
life." Circumstances,-position or possessions, plenty
or poverty, education or illiteracy, prove no barrier
to the blessedness of this experience. Willingness to
conform to the divine condition of "dying with Him"
is the alone necessity. And so it is we find that, even
in regard to this "deepest mystery in the Bible," a little
child may lead us.

It is recorded by Mr. Handley Bird, Missionary in
Madras, that at *ten years of age* his little daughter "Carol"
had the knowledge, and experienced the blessedness,

of being "dead with Christ." In the story of her life Mr. Bird tells us that:

> "When she was but ten years old, dear Carol had great longings to be holy and like her Lord. She became very sensitive of little ways and words that were not lovely, and sought earnestly for deliverance from *self* and every exhibition of the old Carol. We often spent long evenings over the Word, speaking together of the one way of deliverance from sin and *self*, therein so clearly revealed,—a present salvation, here and now, through the death of Jesus for us and *through our union with Him in that death*.

The sixth chapter of Romans, and similar scriptures, were read and prayed over, until the truth of the experience of Galatians 2:20 was released: 'I *am* crucified with Christ.' Of the very real and blessed experience, at this period, of which her mother thus speaks, we have a sweet record in the fly-leaf of her Bible: 'I truly *died with* Jesus, and I put away my old Carol on the cross *with* Him on the 4th of October, 1903, and I mean to live, by His help, for Him all my life, *Not I, but Christ.* This was not when I was converted.'

Fifteen months later came the *outward* 'burial' in her baptism at Teethul, near Bombay, on January 2nd, 1905,-a very solemn and happy event in her spiritual life...Never before had we so realized the force of the words of the Sufferer in the midst of *his* dread Baptism: 'Thy waves and Thy billows are gone over me.' To Carol it was a season of holy delight. Her record in the end of her Bible under this date reads: 'Old Carol was once for all buried with Christ in baptism on the 2nd of January, 1905 Bulsar."

Appropriately, we may add the following verses, which were cherished amongst Carol's "treasures":-

"Except a corn of wheat fall into the ground and *die*, it abideth alone: but if it *die*, it bringeth forth much fruit."

"And *die*? And *die*?
Be buried, planted, sown,
In the fearsome dark alone?

Ah, Lord, it is a better word
My soul hath heard!
'Much fruit' I fain would bear:
But this! canst Thou not spare—
The cross, the grave, the night?
O leave me light!
Is there no other way?
I love the day.

Hush, my beloved,
Come closer to my heart,
That love may strength impart.
'Tis an eternal word
Thy soul hath heard.
It is a royal way—
God's way, Life's way, Love's way.
I could not spare it *me*,
Nor can I thee.
Wilt bide for aye 'alone'
Or for Love's sake be 'sown'?"

This is the vital question. It is very personal. Let it
be repeated—

"Wilt (thou) bide for aye 'alone,'
Or for Love's sake be 'sown'?"

Bishop Taylor Smith, in an opening address at a Keswick convention, has told us how "the question" came to him.

"How well I remember," he said, "on my way to the lake on one occasion many years ago, Mr. Grubb coming up to me and saying: 'Brother, are you willing to be crucified? Are you willing to *die*, for, if you are not, you are no good? You can do nothing until you are dead.' 'Except a corn of wheat fall into the ground and *die* it abideth alone.' So said the Master, Who was the Soil-less Seed in the garner of heaven, and we were the seedless soil, poor fallen humanity, and He was willing to be sown in our flesh that He might bring forth the redeemed to people heaven. And we, following in His steps, must *die* unto sin if we would be raised to newness of life and share the glory which He has promised."

"O Cross, that liftest up my head,
      I dare not ask to fly from thee:
I lay in dust life's glory dead,
     And from the ground there blossoms red
       Life that shall endless be."

Pause now and think! Doubtless you have sung these words‑perhaps quite frequently‑

"I lay in dust Life's glory dead."

Have you truly done so? Then the question is quite in order, "When did *you die?*"

If, hitherto, these words have only been to you a sentimental or a superficial song, realizing now their vital importance, will you not make them to become a solemn, a sober and a sweet reality, and do it *now!*

"I lay in dust Life's glory *dead*."

Then shall you find that:‑

"from the ground there blossoms red
      Life that shall endless be."

THE SOUL'S RESPONSE

He said: "Wilt thou go with Me
Where shadows eclipse the light?"
And she answered: "My Lord, I will follow Thee
Far under the stars of night."
But He said: "No starlight pierces the gloom
Of the valley thy feet must tread;
But it leads thee on to a cross and tomb-"
"But I go with Thee," she said.

"Count the cost-canst thou pay the price,-
Be as a dumb thing led;
Laid on an altar of sacrifice?"
"Bind me there, my Lord," she said.
"Bind, that I may not fail-
Or hold with Thy wounded hand;
For I fear the knife and the piercing nail,
And I shrink from the burning brand.
Yet whither Thou goest I will go,
Though the way be lone and dread-"
His voice was tender, and sweet, and low,-
"Thou shalt go with Me," He said.

And none knew the anguish sore
Or the night of the way she came;
Alone, alone with the cross she bore,
Alone in her grief and shame.
Brought to the altar of sacrifice,
There as a dumb thing slain:
Was the guerdon more than the bitter price?
Was it worth the loss and pain?

Ask the seed-com, when the grain
Ripples its ripened gold;
Ask the sower when, after toil and pain,
He garners the hundred-fold.
He said (and His voice was glad and sweet):
"Was it worth the cost, My own?"
And she answered, low at His pierced feet,
"I found at the end of the pathway lone
Not death, but life on a throne!"

(Annie Clarke)

If it die it bringeth forth much fruit." "If It Die!"

"All through life I see a cross,
Where sons of God yield up their breath
There is no gain except by loss,
There is no life *except by death*."

(Walter C. Smith, D.D.)

How to
Die Daily

B. McCall Barbour

Copyright March 2013

Reprinted *with* Permission *from*
Theodore C. Danson Smith

CROWN
CHRISTIAN
PUBLICATIONS
Royal Reading

FaithfortheFamily.com

Book 2

HOW *to* DIE DAILY

To "die daily" we must live divinely. Also, let it be noted, there can be no true experience of "dying daily" where there is no intelligent sense of having previously, by faith, died *definitely*. "Verily, verily, I say unto you, Except a corn of wheat fall into the ground and die, it abideth alone: but if it die, it bringeth forth much fruit" (John 12:24). These are fundamental principles of the faith which should not be ignored. Therefore the reason, as well as the necessity, for pressing home upon every believer in Christ a previous question, "When did *you* die?"

By "died definitely" we mean that there must have taken place a decided transaction of *identification with Christ* in His crucifixion on the cross, in His burial in the grave, and in His resurrection. Paul clearly expresses it thus in the familiar phrase—so commonly quoted, but so seldom understood or realized in experience—"I am crucified with Christ: nevertheless I live; yet not I, but Christ liveth in me: and the life which I now live in the flesh I live by the faith of the Son of God, who loved me, and gave himself for me" (Galatians 2:20).

It is the plan, as it also is the provision of God, that every blood-bought child of His may, as He has purposed they should, "walk in newness of life" (Romans 6:4). Let it be empasized that there can be no true, practical experience of walking in "the power of His resurrection" (Philippians 3:10), and in "newness of life," where there has been no previous personal experience of identification with Christ in His crucifixion—in "dying with Jesus." Beloved, with sincere affection we would entreat you to face this all-important question, "When did *you* die?" when, by faith, our "dying with Jesus" and our burial with Him have been decided—when these steps are accomplished in our experience, *then* our rising with Him (Colossians 2:12) may also be reckoned upon, and its blessedness may be realized in our life.

Thus, appropriating "the power of His resurrection," and thereby experiencing His perpetual presence; being "alive unto God" (Romans 6:11) and yielding our whole being to Him; it is made possible for us, personally and practically, to "die daily" unto self. "Know ye not, that so many of us as were baptized into Jesus Christ were baptized into his death? Therefore we are buried with him by baptism into death: that like as Christ was raised up from the dead by the glory of the Father, *even so we also* should walk in newness of life" (Romans 6:3-4).

True walking with Christ is true Christian conduct, which results only from true Christian character. That character is, "Christ, who is our life" (Colossians 3:4). "I live; yet not I, but Christ liveth in me" (Galatians 2:20)

It is soundest wisdom to face the fact that it is absolutely futile to attempt to walk in the ways of God otherwise than according to His ways, as is revealed in His infallible Word. His way to "dying *daily*" is by first, by faith, *dying definitely*. Thereafter it is possible to *walk divinely* with Him. "I will dwell in them, and walk in them" (II Corinthians 6:16). There need be no problem or perplexity regarding this, to the sincere seeker after truth, if only the Word of God be heard, and heeded, and obeyed. The Holy Spirit is "given to them that obey Him" (Acts 5:32), and He is given, for one thing, to guide—"He will guide you into all truth" (John 16:13). "If any man will do his will, he shall know of the doctrine" (John 7:17).

Shall we, then, listen to His Word even now?

> *"For the love of Christ constraineth us;*
> *because we thus judge, that if one died for*
> *all, then were all dead: And that he died*
> *for all, that they which live should not*
> *henceforth live unto themselves, but unto*
> *him which died for them, and rose again."*
> (II Corinthians 5:14-15)

In the light of this divine pronouncement, we are better able to understand the overmastering passion of Paul when he says:—

> *But what things were gain to me, those I*
> *counted loss for Christ. Yea doubtless, and*
> *I count all things but loss for the excellency*

of the knowledge of Christ Jesus my Lord: for whom I have suffered the loss of all things, and do count them but dung, that I may win Christ, And be found in him, not having mine own righteousness, which is of the law, but that which is through the faith of Christ, the righteousness which is of God by faith: That I may know him, and the power of his resurrection, and the fellowship of his sufferings, being made conformable unto his death; If by any means I might attain unto the resurrection of the dead.

Not as though I had already attained, either were already perfect: but I follow after, if that I may apprehend that for which also I am apprehended of Christ Jesus. Brethren, I count not myself to have apprehended: but this one thing I do, forgetting those things which are behind, and reaching forth unto those things which are before, I press toward the mark for the prize of the high calling of God in Christ

Jesus. Let us therefore, as many as be perfect, be thus minded: and if in any thing ye be otherwise minded, God shall reveal even this unto you. Nevertheless, whereto we have already attained, let us walk by the same rule, let us mind the same thing.

(Philippians 3:7-16)

Now then, having settled it that we have, by faith, and according to the terms of Scripture, definitely identified ourselves with Christ in His crucifixion, death, burial, and resurrection, we may now, as the Apostle exhorts, "persevere in the same course." That "same course" presents to us the further step of the subject under view, *viz.*, how to "die *daily*." The attitude of identification with Christ in His crucifixion, etc., has now to be manifested in the act and fact of "dying daily."

'Buried with Christ,' and raised with Him, too;
What is there left for me to do?
Simply to cease from struggling and strife,
Simply to 'walk in newness of life.'

'Risen with Christ,'-my glorious Head,
Holiness now the pathway I tread,
Beautiful thought, while walking therein:
'He that is dead is freed from sin.'

'Living with Christ,' Who 'dieth no more,'
Following Christ, Who goeth before;
I am from bondage utterly freed,
Reckoning self as 'dead indeed.'

Living for Christ, my members I yield
Servants to God for evermore sealed;
'Not under Law,' I'm now 'under grace';
Sin is dethroned, and Christ takes its place.

Growing in Christ; no more shall be named
Things of which now I'm truly ashamed;
'Fruit unto holiness' will I bear;
Life evermore the end I shall share.

(Rev. T. Ryder)

"More and more," says Dr. A.C. Gaebelein, "it has
come to my heart and mind that, in these solemn days,
so pregnant with meaning for the true church, we, too,

must enter deeper into this great confession of the Apostle Paul and *live that life which is dead to sin and dead to the world.* It does not mean a sinless or a perfect life. Far from that! *Daily* we must do it afresh, *yielding ourselves unto God* as those that are alive from the dead, and present our bodies a living sacrifice unto God. If the glorious fact that He 'died for our sins,' that our sins can no longer rise up against us, brings joy and peace, the life that realizes in faith the death to sin and the world, through the death of Christ, brings a still greater joy and peace, as well as the assurance that we please God."

"What is there left for me to do?" The answer is–To 'die daily.'" "How?" you ask. By reckoning yourself to be dead indeed unto sin, but alive unto God through Jesus Christ our Lord (Romans 6:11).

> *"Let not sin therefore reign in your mortal body, that ye should obey it in the lusts thereof. Neither yield ye your members as instruments of unrighteousness unto sin: but yield yourselves unto God, as those that are alive from the dead, and your members as instruments of righteousness unto God."*
> (Romans 6:12-13)

Let it be emphasized. "Yield yourselves unto God." "Yourselves!" "Yourselves!!"

"There are many persons," writes the Rev. Marcus Rainsford, "who, as far as we can judge by their conduct, and by their conversation, yield their *members* to righteousness. It is marvellous how much good some people do. There is rarely a work of charity in which they are not engaged. There is rarely a work of mercy in which they are not busied, and in which they do not participate.

Schools are watched over, the poor are visited; it is wonderful the ramifications of usefulness which some *professing* Christians gather around them. But, they may do all that, and *not yield their own selves to God.* My dear friends, I have known, during my ministry, many whose whole life was spent in acts of kindness and sympathy, and in tender compassion for the sufferings and the wants of others, whose *hearts were never given to God.*

Satan is very cunning; he will allow you to be as *religious* as you please, and as charitable as you like; will let you undergo any amount of privation, and give you leave to extend to the need around you, any amount of help, *as long as you keep 'yourselves' from God.* The Apostle, by the Spirit of God, puts this truth before us:–Yield *yourselves* and then your members. This is what he also says in II Corinthians 8:5. The Corinthians '*first* gave their own selves to the Lord,' and then to His service...The truth is the believer is Christ's portion. We are His by creation; His as the Father's gift to Him. We are His by purchase; bought by His blood. We are His–thank God! By the voluntary surrender of our hearts to Him; and, as we realize that we are His, we shall give *ourselves* first to Him, and next to *His service.* For the life that Christ now lives, He lives unto God: and if we are in participation with that life, we cannot live devoting our members to the service of Satan."

"Yield *yourselves* unto God!!"

Here it is good that we should remind ourselves of the stated truth that *we are not our own,* but that we are the property of Christ.

"What? know ye not that your body is the temple of the Holy Ghost which is in you, which ye have of God, and ye are not your own? For ye are bought with a price: therefore glorify God in your body, and in your spirit, which are God's" (I Corinthians 6:19-20).

Have you "yielded" to Him His property? Have you, dear reader, given *yourself* to Him?

A very poor man lived alone in a little hut. The poor man decided to sell it, and went about the place patching the roof and repairing it carefully, feeling a sense of pride that the rich man should desire his hut. After the money was paid, the new owner began at once to tear down the shack. The poor, bewildered man remonstrated with him. "Don't tear down my dear little home. I have repaired it all so nicely." But the wealthy man replied, "I do not want your *shack*: I only want the *site*, the corner lot." It is not our "shack," patched up by the energy of the flesh, that our Lord desires from any of us. It is the "site"-"ourselves"-He wants; and has all right to; that He may build thereon the fair fabric of His "new creation," and so manifest to men His life, not ours. Friend, let Him have "*yourself*"!

> "'No longer I, but Christ.' O precious Lord,
> How can I speak the sweetness of this word,
> By which from bondage Thou hast set me free,
> Giving me perfect liberty in Thee.
> 'No longer I, but Christ'-then am I 'dead';

'Buried,' yet risen in my glorious Head;
'Buried,' that self no longer come between
His love and souls. Henceforth be only seen
The beauty and the glory of my Lord
Upon His child:-His power in every word,
His life in every act, and look and tone;
Mine the sweet peace, the glory His alone.
'No longer I.' When comes temptation's hour,
His is the kingdom, therefore His the power;
He knoweth how to keep in perfect peace
The soul in which His reign doth never cease.
'No longer I, but Christ,'-may not choose,
But follow each command, nor e'er refuse
A call to service, whatsoe'er it be,
For *Jesus* calls and is enough for me.
O life of sweetest liberty so blest,
I *yield Him all*, and He does all the rest."

(Freda Hanbury Allan)

"'Buried with Christ,' and raised with Him, too;
What is there left for me to do?"

For answer, we would say *four things*. These four
things may be summarized in four words,-Power,
Pattern, Purpose, and Practice.

THE POWER

First, then, let there be appropriation, by faith, of "the Power of His resurrection." This is the *only* power that can perform the obligations, and produce the desired results; the only power that can enable us to "live divinely" unto God, and so "die daily" unto self. Thus it is that Paul, so passionately interested in the spiritual growth of the saints at Ephesus, and, by implication, in all saints everywhere, prays:

> *"That the God of our Lord Jesus Christ, the Father of glory, may give unto you the spirit of wisdom and revelation in the knowledge of him: The eyes of your understanding being enlightened; that ye may know what is the hope of his calling, and what the riches of the glory of his inheritance in the saints, And what is the exceeding greatness of his power to us-ward who believe, according to the working of his mighty power,*

Which he wrought in Christ, when he raised him from the dead, and set him at his own right hand in the heavenly places, Far above all principality, and power, and might, and dominion, and every name that is named, not only in this world, but also in that which is to come: And hath put all things under his feet, and gave him to be the head over all things to the church, Which is his body, the fullness of him that filleth all in all."

(Ephesians 1:17-23)

Such is "the power of His resurrection." This power is alone in Christ. "Christ the power of God" (I Corinthians 1:24). Amazing fact-his overcoming power is also "in us believers" who appropriate Him as our life.

"With *life* in Christ," writes the editor of *The Christian*, "the Christian is meant to have *power*. By union with Him, the *power* is guaranteed no less than the life. When He said that He came that we might have life, He meant life in its fullness-life that is characterized by this power–by *His* power. The resurrection life of Christ our Lord is available for those who are 'risen with Christ'; and that life is a life of power, of liberty, of victory, of joy, of fruitfulness, of soul-saving and soul-blessing intercourse with others–not through anything in the human instrument, but through the power of Christ working in the instrument.

Power was the subject of one of His great post-resurrection promises. 'Ye shall receive power, after that the Holy Ghost is come upon you.' But *it is possible to have life without power*: and paralysis is only less terrible than death itself. Are we paralyzed? He can heal this paralysis of spiritual life and usefulness. He–and He alone–can say, 'Arise, take up thy bed and walk.'"

"Faithful is he that calleth you, who also will do it" (I Thessalonians 5:24).

> "My strength is weakness, but Thy power is might,
> And makes me strong to battle for the right."

> New power to live as Christ would have us live;
> Because He comes anew to dwell within;
> New vigour, quickened faith, and warmer love;
> That makes us hate the very thought of sin.

This, this, the life He waiteth to impart,
To those who yield an undivided heart."
(Mary E. Kendrew)

"What shall *we*, then, say to these things?" Shall it be:-

I take Thee, blessed Lord;
I give myself to Thee;
And Thou, according to Thy Word,
Dost undertake for me."
(Rev. A.B. Simpson)

"'Buried with Christ,' and raised with Him, too;
What is there left for me to do?"

THE PATTERN

Let there be guidance by the Pattern of the Christ-life.

Note carefully the word that is used is "*Guidance*," not "Imitation." We are not called to imitate the life of Christ. We are not, by efforts of our own, to try to *copy* Him. As, henceforth, "for me to live is Christ," our supreme business is to *let Him live*. We are called to let Him reproduce His own life in us and through us. As one has very aptly said, "This risen life is not the imitation of a splendid model, but *the indwelling of a living Person.* The Christ-life is only the outward development of the Christ nature; the life manifesting itself after it's kind. Personal and abiding union with Him makes it as easy for the believer to do Christ-like works, as for the branch to bear the luscious fruit when it is in unhindered fellowship with the vine."

He left us an example that we should follow His steps (I Peter 2:21). The example (pattern) of "His steps" has been left to us that, as we follow Him, we may definitely know our steps are in correct conformity with His own, so that we may "walk, even as He walked" (I John 2:6). There need be no confusion concerning either Himself as the " power" for the life or as its "pattern." And the pathway of "His steps" is definitely defined in His own Word. "Thy word is a lamp unto my feet, and a light unto my path" (Psalm 119:105). The way He went was "the way of the Cross." There is *no other way.* It must not be avoided by any who would follow faithfully in "His steps." This is true discipleship, and herein do we find "the fellowship of His sufferings."

"For even hereunto were ye called: because Christ also suffered for us, leaving us an example, that ye should follow his steps: Who did no sin, neither was guile found in his mouth: Who, when he was reviled, reviled not again; when he suffered, he threatened not; but committed himself to him that judgeth righteously: Who his own self bare our sins in his own body on the tree, that we, being dead to sins, should live unto righteousness: by whose stripes ye were healed."

(I Peter 2:21-24)

This, we repeat, is discipleship indeed (John 8:31). The words of Jesus himself have left us in no doubt about this.

"If any man come to me, and hate not his father, and mother, and wife, and children, and brethren, and sisters, yea, and his own life also, he cannot be my disciple. And whosoever doth not bear his cross, and come after me, cannot be my disciple."

(Luke 14:26-27)

"So likewise, whosoever he be of you that forsaketh not all that he hath, he cannot be my disciple."

(Luke 14:33)

We would affectionately direct attention to the thrice-repeated "cannot" in these injunctions, and emphasize the fact that it is Christ himself who says it. "If ye love me, keep my commandments" (John 14:15).

Commenting on these scriptures, Dr. Campbell Morgan has said:-"The *new relationship* must be superior, in the urgency of its claims, to the claim of any *earthly* relationship; it must be considered and answered *before any claims of the self-life*. The teacher demands that we take up the cross and so follow on, even though the progress be through pain: More-we must take the deep spiritual vow of poverty, renouncing all as possessions, counting every word He shall speak, and every truth He shall reveal, through whatever methods, as our chief and only wealth. In short, we must not be held, either by being possessed by others or possessing aught. There must be a clean severance from all entanglement, and an utter uncompromising abandonment of ourselves to Him. Unless this is so we *cannot* be His disciples.

If these conditions seem hard and severe, let it be remembered what depends upon them; character and destiny depend upon this question of discipleship. Not to impart information, and to satisfy curiosity, is Jesus the teacher. It is because the truth sanctifies and makes free that He reveals it, and because, apart from the revelation He has to make, *there is no possible way of revealing God's great purposes for us.* Compare Himself and His teaching with the most sacred and beautiful of earth's lives and possessions, and these are unworthy of a moment's thought. They must all come from between Him and ourselves that so we may know and do His will. Such attitude does not rob us of the enjoyment of all these things, so far as in themselves they are right. It rather adds to our joy.

Self renders it impossible to know Christ when other lives and interests intervene, and breeds dissatisfaction with all else, and makes that very self sad and weak. Christ absolute, lights the whole being with His love and joy and beauty, and shines on other lives to their sanctification, and so the abnegation of self is self's highest development."

For the obliteration of self there must be absolute abandonment to Christ, even to the "dying as He died." "Looking unto Jesus the author and finisher of our faith; who for the joy that was set before him endured the cross, despising the shame, and is set down at the right hand of the throne of God. For consider him that endured such contradiction of sinners against himself, lest ye be wearied and faint in your minds." (Hebrew 12:2-3). "Consider Him!"

> "A homeless Stranger amongst us came,
> To this land of death and mourning;
> He walked in a path of sorrow and shame,
> Through insult, and hate, and scorning.
>
> A Man of Sorrows, of toil, of tears,
> An outcast Man and a lonely;
> But He looked on me, and through endless years
> Him must I love—Him only."

However severe may be "the fellowship of His sufferings," priceless, indeed, is it to have such a privilege, and unspeakable are the compensations of such a partnership with Him. "And if children, then heirs; heirs of God, and *joint-heirs* with Christ; *if so be* that we suffer with him, that we may be also glorified together" (Romans 8:17).

> Then afar and afar did I follow Him on
> To the land where He was going—
> To the depths of glory beyond the sun
> Where the golden fields were glowing—
>
> The golden harvest of endless joy,
> The joy He had sown in weeping;
> How can I tell the blest employ,
> The songs of the glorious reaping.
>
> The recompense sweet, the full reward,
> Which the Lord, His God, has given;
> At rest beneath the wings of the Lord,
> At home in the courts of heaven."

(P.G.)

*"And when he had called the people unto
him with his disciples also, he said unto
them, Whosoever will come after me, let
him deny himself, and take up his cross,
and follow me. For whosoever will save his
life shall lose it; but whosoever shall lose his
life for my sake and the gospel's, the same
shall save it. For what shall it profit a man,
if he shall gain the whole world, and lose
his own soul? Or what shall a man give in
exchange for his soul?"*

(Mark 8:34-37)

Beloved, we beseech you, do not dismiss these sayings
of Jesus with indifference or neglect. We affectionately
commend, for your prayerful consideration, the
following impressive comments bearing on this theme
by Mr. W. J. Irvine, for all who would be "disciples
indeed." He writes:—"Our natural lives seldom exceed
threescore years and ten; and in these lie opportunity
to be faithful and loyal to Him Who loved us and gave
Himself for us. *The danger lies in wasting this life by living
for self and the world.* The reserve that would spare this
life from suffering *for His sake,* is the cause of a lost

life. The loyalty that puts Christ first, even in the face of the loss of all, even life itself, finds its reward in a 'saved' life. 'Who redeemeth thy life from destruction' follows 'who forgiveth all iniquities' (Psalm 103:3-4). In proportion as our lives are surrendered to Him, and filled with His Holy Spirit, in that proportion will we realize that salvation of which our Lord here speaks. A saved life is incomparably better than a world gained, and *nothing the world can give can profit the man who fails to follow Christ*."

> If I find Him, if I follow,
> What His guerdon here?
> Many a sorrow, many a labour, many a tear!
>
> If I still hold closely to Him,
> What hath He at last?
> Sorrow vanquished, labour ended, tears are past.
>
> Finding, following, keeping, trusting,
> Is He sure to bless?
> Saints, apostles, prophets, martyrs, answer Yes!"

That we be not deceived by the subtlety of the enemy of our souls, there is need for discerning the distinction and difference between the troubles and trials, the problems and perplexities of our ordinary human life, that we call "our cross," and "the cross" we are called to bear *with* and *for* Christ in "the fellowship of His sufferings." "And he that *taketh* not his cross, and followeth after me, is not worthy of me" (Matthew 10:38).

Listen!

"My cross is not the thing I share in common
    With all the travellers along life's road
The certain lot of every man and woman,
    The sudden sorrow, or the daily load.

This flesh is heir to many ills, and truly,
    As sparks fly upward, come distress and loss,
Change and defeat, and disappointment duly-
    But these things in themselves are not-My cross.'

'If any man will serve Me,' saith the Master,
    'He must take up his cross and follow Me;
Who so would shrink from suffering and disaster,
    In no true sense can My disciple be.'

My cross is something I am only bearing
    Because I follow Christ; forsaking all;
Something I could refuse, or shirk, uncaring,
    Did I not answer to His Love's sweet call!

My cross—like His—means death by crucifixion
    To this or that thing, as the case may be;
Self-abnegation and self-contradiction,
    That Christ thereby be magnified in me.

I would not shun my cross, nor crave exemption;
    Reveal Thy crimsoned foot-prints, Lord, to me;
Make me more worthy of Thy great Redemption;
    Help me with strong desire to follow Thee!"
                (Winifred A. Iverson)

It will spare us much heart-burning, and heart-breaking, to recognize and to remember that "the way of the Cross" is *never* the way of self-seeking, self-serving, or self-pleasing. Never! It ever is the pathway of self-sacrifice for the sake of others for their good, and of loving surrender of self to the will of God for His glory. "And whosoever of you will be the chiefest, shall be the servant of all. For even the Son of Man came *not to be ministered* unto, but to minister, and to give his life a ransom for many" (Mark 10:44-45). "Let this mind be in you, which was also in Christ Jesus" (Philippians 2:5). "My sheep hear my voice, and I know them, and they follow me" (John 10:27).

"O Jesus, I have promised
    To serve Thee to the end;
Be Thou for ever near me,
    My Master and my Friend:
I shall not fear the battle
    If Thou art by my side,
Nor wander from the pathway
    If Thou wilt be my Guide.

Oh, let me hear Thee speaking,
    In accents clear and still,
Above the storms of passion,
    The murmurs of self-will.
Oh speak, to reassure me,
    To hasten or control;
Oh speak, and make me listen,
    Thou Guardian of my soul!

Oh, let me see Thy footmarks,
　　And in them plant mine own;
My hope to follow duly
　　Is in Thy strength alone.
Oh, guide me, call me, draw me,
　　Uphold me to the end;
And then in heaven receive me,
　　My Saviour and my Friend."

(John E. Bode)

"'Buried with Christ,' and raised with Him, too;
What is there left for me to do?"

THE PURPOSE

Let there be a definite understanding of the Purpose for "dying daily."

To know this purpose is to know the will of God. To know God's will is a necessary condition of mind to the fullest working-out of "the power of His resurrection" in us, in co-operation with Him in "the fellowship of His sufferings," and our walk with Him in "newness of life." Simply and scripturally stated, the purpose of God in our "dying daily" to self, is, "that the life of Jesus might be made manifest in our mortal flesh" (II Corinthians 4:11). Beloved friend, has this divine purpose been gripped by you? Have you been gripped by it?

> *"For we preach not ourselves, but Christ Jesus the Lord; and ourselves your servants for Jesus' sake. For God, who commanded the light to shine out of darkness, hath shined in our hearts, to give the light of the knowledge of the glory of God in the face of Jesus Christ. But we have this treasure in earthen vessels, that the excellency of the power may be of God, and not of us.*
>
> *We are troubled on every side, yet not distressed; we are perplexed, but not in despair; Persecuted, but not forsaken; cast down, but not destroyed; Always bearing about in the body the dying of the Lord Jesus, that the life also of Jesus might be made manifest in our body. For we which live are always delivered unto death for Jesus' sake, that the life also of Jesus might*

be made manifest in our mortal flesh. So
then death worketh in us, but life in you."

(II Corinthians 4:5-12)

"God in heaven hath a treasure,
    Riches none may count or tell;
Hath a deep eternal pleasure,
    Christ, the Son, He loveth well.
God hath here on earth a treasure,
    None but He its price may know
Deep, unfathomable pleasure,
    Christ revealed in saints below.

Oh to be but emptier, lowlier,
    Mean, unnoticed, and unknown,
And to God a vessel holier,
    Filled with Christ and Christ alone!
Naught of earth to cloud the glory,
    Naught of self the light to dim,
Telling forth His wondrous story,
    Emptied to be filled with Him."

"But ye shall receive power, after that the Holy Ghost is come upon you: and ye shall be witnesses unto me both in Jerusalem, and in all Judaea, and in Samaria, and unto the uttermost part of the earth."

(Acts 1:8)

"For the life was manifested, and we have seen it, and bear witness, and shew unto you that eternal life, which was with the Father, and was manifested unto us;) That which we have seen and heard declare we unto you, that ye also may have fellowship with us: and truly our fellowship is with the Father, and with his Son Jesus Christ. And these things write we unto you, that your joy may be full."

(I John 1:2-4)

"Channels only, blessed Master,
    Yet with all Thy wondrous power
Flowing through us, Thou canst use us
    Every day and every hour.

Witnessing Thy power to save me;
    Setting free from self and sin;
Thou hast bought me to possess me;
    In Thy fullness, Lord, come in!"

> "Ye are our epistle written in our hearts, known and read of all men: Forasmuch as ye are manifestly declared to be the epistle of Christ ministered by us, written not with ink, but with the Spirit of the living God; not in tables of stone, but in fleshy tables of the heart."

(II Corinthians 3:2-3)

"We are the only Bible
    The careless world will read;
We are the sinner's gospel,
    We are the scoffer's creed.
We are the Lord's last message,
    Given in deed and word:
What if the type is crooked?
    What if the print is blurred?"

"Wherefore, my beloved, as ye have always obeyed, not as in my presence only, but now much more in my absence, work out your own salvation with fear and trembling. For it is God which worketh in you both to will and to do of his good pleasure. Do all things without murmurings and disputings: That ye may be blameless and harmless, the sons of God, without rebuke, in the midst of a crooked and perverse nation, among whom ye shine as lights in the world; Holding forth the word of life; that I may rejoice in the day of Christ, that I have not run in vain, neither laboured in vain."

(Philippians 2:12-16)

"Christ has no hands but our hands
　　To do His work to-day ;
He has no feet but our feet
　　To lead men in His way.
He has no tongue but our tongue
　　To tell men how He died ;
He has no help but our help,
　　To bring them to His side."

"Let your light so shine before men, that they may see your good works, and glorify your Father which is in heaven" (Matthew 5:16).

> "His lamp am I,
> To shine where He shall say:
> And lamps are not for sunny rooms,
> Nor for the light of day.
> But for dark places of the earth,
> Where shame and crime and wrong have been;
> Or for the murky twilight grey,
> Where wandering sheep have gone astray,
> Or where the light of faith grows dim,
> And souls are groping after Him.
> And so, sometimes a flame we find,
> Clear shining through the night,
> So bright we do not see the lamp
> But only see the light.
> So may I shine–His life the flame
> That men may glorify His name."
>
> (Annie Johnson Flint)

"As thou hast sent me into the world, even so have I also sent them into the world. And for their sakes I sanctify myself, that they also might

be sanctified through the truth. Neither pray I for these alone, but for them also which shall believe on me through their word; That they all may be one; as thou, Father, art in me, and I in thee, that they also may be one in us: that the world may believe that thou hast sent me.

And the glory which thou gavest me I have given them; that they may be one, even as we are one: I in them, and thou in me, that they may be made perfect in one; and that the world may know that thou hast sent me, and hast loved them, as thou hast loved me."

(John 17:18-23)

"Live out Thy life within me,
    O Jesus, King of kings!
Be Thou Thyself the answer
    To all my questionings.
Live out Thy life within me,
    In all things have Thy way!
I, the transparent medium,
    Thy glory to display."

"*According to my earnest expectation and my hope, that in nothing I shall be ashamed, but that with all boldness, as always, so now also Christ shall be magnified in my body, whether it be by life, or by death. For to me to live is Christ, and to die is gain.*"

(Philippians 1:20-21)

"*I am crucified with Christ: nevertheless I live; yet not I, but Christ liveth in me: and the life which I now live in the flesh I live by the faith of the Son of God, who loved me, and gave himself for me.*"

(Galatians 2:20)

"Not I, but Christ, be honoured, loved, exalted,
Not I, but Christ, be seen, be known, be heard,
Not I, but Christ, in every look and action,
Not I, but Christ, in every thought and word."

"*But God forbid that I should glory, save in the cross of our Lord Jesus Christ, by whom the world is crucified unto me,*"

*and I unto the world. For in Christ Jesus
neither circumcision availeth any thing,
nor uncircumcision, but a new creature.
And as many as walk according to this
rule, peace be on them, and mercy, and
upon the Israel of God."*

(Galatians 6:14-16)

*"Now thanks be unto God, which always
causeth us to triumph in Christ, and maketh
manifest the savour of his knowledge by us
in every place"*

(II Corinthians 2:14).

"I am crucified with Jesus,
    And the Cross hath set me free;
I have risen again with Jesus,
    And He lives and reigns in me.

This the story of the Master,
    Through the Cross He reached the Throne;
And, like Him, our path to glory
    Ever leads through death alone."

"'Buried with Christ,' and raised with Him, too;
    What is there left for me to do?
Simply to cease from struggling and strife,
    Simply to 'walk in newness of life.'"

THE PRACTICE

Let there be the daily Practice of the Presence of Christ as the life. "I will dwell in them, and walk in them" (II Corinthians 6:16). "This I say then, Walk in the Spirit, and ye shall not fulfill the lust of the flesh" (Galatians 5:16). Logical reasoning at once admits that, if the former–"walking in the Spirit"–is enacted, the latter–"fulfilling the lust of the flesh"–will be averted. There is no other way by which this happy result can be achieved. If, for any reason, we fail to "walk in the Spirit," there is no other course open for the time being but to live in the flesh.

The choice, therefore, is set before every true child of God. The entire lack of any alternative course emphasizes the truth that if we would "die daily" to self, daily we must "walk divinely." Absolute abandonment to Christ as our life can alone accomplish the obliteration of "self." In stating this we would add a word of warning, in the simple, yet profound remark of another, "This, I know, whatever degree of being dead is possible, we are always alive enough to be able to return into our self. Our life must always be an 'overcoming' one. The promise is 'to him that overcometh' (Revelation 3:21). This is gloriously possible, and the secret is-himself."

We are instructed by the Scriptures to recognize the possibility of the uprising of "the flesh," and we are likewise instructed to "mortify" (make dead) the members of the body (Colossians 3:5). There is no suggestion, however, in this, that we are to *kill*, to persecute, or to punish ourselves. The divine method is to "reckon ye yourselves to be dead," and to treat the self-life so.

We are to act towards ourselves-towards the self-life-as we would act toward a corpse. We are to "put on the Lord Jesus Christ, and make not provision for the flesh, to fulfill the lusts thereof" (Romans 13:14). When the flesh would seek to assert itself, let the divine injunction be remembered and acted upon. "Likewise reckon ye also yourselves to be dead indeed unto sin, but alive unto God through Jesus Christ our Lord" (Romans 6:11). Instantly relegate the fleshly desire, inclination, or passion to the grave, to which, with "the old man," these belong, and "yield yourselves unto God, as those that are alive from the dead, and your members as instruments of righteousness unto God" (Romans 6:13).

So serious, and so disastrous are the consequences to ourselves, and to others, when the "flesh" is yielded to, that our Lord Himself has warned us, that if our eye, our hand, or our feet offend–stumble ourselves or others–it is better these should be "cast out" or "cut off" than cause such disaster. But, oh, friend, there is a still better way than that of such devastating treatment of the members of our body. Yea, there is a way that is *best*. "I beseech you therefore, brethren, by the mercies of God, that ye present your bodies a *living sacrifice*, holy, acceptable unto God, which is your reasonable service. And be not conformed to this world: but be ye transformed by the renewing of your mind, that ye may prove what is that good, and acceptable, and perfect, will of God" (Romans 12:1-2). "If ye, through the Spirit, do mortify the deeds of the body, ye shall live" (Romans 8:13). In reference to this, Dr. A.B. Simpson very forcibly says, "The Holy Spirit is the only One who can *kill us and keep us dead.*

Many Christians try to do this disagreeable work themselves, and they are going through a continual crucifixion, but they can never accomplish the work permanently. This is the work of the Holy Spirit; and when you really yield yourself to the death, it is delightful to find how sweetly He can slay you...It is not the work of man nor means, nor of our own strugglings, but His own prerogative.

It is divine holiness, not human self improvement or perfection. It is the inflow, into man's being, of the life of and purity of the Infinite, Eternal Holy One, bringing His own perfection, and working out in us, His own will. How easy, how spontaneous, how delightful, this heavenly way of holiness! Surely it is a "highway" (Isaiah 35:8), and not the low way of man's vain and fruitless mortification.

It is God's great elevated railway, sweeping over the heads of the struggling throngs who toil along the lower pavement, when they might be borne along on the ascension pathway by His own almighty impulse. It is

God's great elevator, carrying us up to the higher chambers of His palace without our laborious efforts, while others struggle up the winding stair and faint by the way. It is God's great tidal wave, bearing up the stranded ship until she floats above the bar without straining timbers or struggling seamen, instead of the ineffectual and tiresome efforts of the struggling crew and the steam of the engines, which had tried in vain to move her an inch, until the heavenly impulse lifted her by its own attraction.

It is God's great law of gravitation, lifting up, by the warm sunbeams, the mighty iceberg, which a million men could not raise a single inch, but which melts away before the warmth of the sunshine, and rises in clouds of evaporation to meet its embrace, until the cold and heavy mass is floating in fleecy clouds of glory in the blue ocean of the sky. How easy all this! How mighty! How simple! How divine! Beloved, have you come into this divine way of holiness?

If you have, how your heart must swell with gratitude as it echoes the truth of the words you have just read! If you have not, do you not long for it, and will you not now unite in the prayer that the very God of peace sanctify you wholly?"

"I've reckoned myself to be dead unto sin,
And risen with Christ and now He lives within,
The life more abundant He gives unto me,
This overflow life gives me full victory."

*"If ye then be risen with Christ, seek those
things which are above, where Christ sitteth on
the right hand of God. Set your affection on
things above, not on things on the earth. For
ye are dead, and your life is hid with Christ
in God. When Christ, who is our life, shall
appear, then shall ye also appear with him in
glory. Mortify therefore your members which
are upon the earth; fornication, uncleanness,
inordinate affection, evil concupiscence, and
covetousness, which is idolatry."*

(Colossians 3:1-5)

*"And they that are Christ's have crucified
the flesh with the affections and lusts. If
we live in the Spirit, let us also walk in the
Spirit. Let us not be desirous of vain glory,
provoking one another, envying one another."*

(Galatians 5:24-26)

"Redeemed by Christ, Who died for me,
  For Him 'tis now to live;
By grace divine, from death made free,
  To Christ the life we give.

In every action here below,
  The Lord to sanctify:
The motive now in all we do—
  His Name to magnify.

One cherished sin within the heart,
  One evil thought received—
The joy of Christ must needs depart,
  The Holy Spirit grieved.

O Holy Spirit, have Thy way!
  The power Thou must supply;
Our hearts and wills we yield to Thee
  Our God to glorify."

Such, then, is the practice of "dying daily." Some incidents of its outworking, in the experiences of the daily life, may be profitable in making what has been said about its "practice" still more plain.

It is recorded of a blacksmith that, after his conversion, he was arrested by the text, "Whether therefore ye eat, or drink, or whatsoever ye do, do all to the glory of God" (I Corinthians 10:31). All that the words meant he did not at first understand. But there were three conclusions that came to his mind, as legitimate deductions from them.

1. That all things that are right to do can be done to God's glory.

2. That whatever might not glorify God had better not be touched.

3. That that was of most value which glorifies God most.

The word "glory" did not much disturb him, for he defined it in a very practical way. "To glorify God," he said, "is to represent Him, so that everybody will think better of Him than before." Accordingly, he resolved that he would make this text the motto of his life. Almost at once he was conscious of the immediate presence of God. The next morning, as he sat down to breakfast, he repeated to himself the text: "Whether ye eat, or drink, or whatsoever ye do, do all to the glory of God." He said to himself: "I will eat this food to the glory of God." His wife noticed that her husband did not eat as fast as usual, and that he was more careful of what he ate than had been his practice. She did not forget, either, that he thanked her for preparing the meal, and had no criticism to make on the coffee.

After prayers he went to his shop, reminding himself that he had promised a farmer to repair his plough-coulter that forenoon. He did not forget that he used to do his work when he pleased, and without special motive, except the money he got out of it. He went to work in the morning saying: "I will mend that plough-coulter for the glory of God." How careful he was to get just the right heat, and, when the steel came out of the forge ready for the anvil, he turned it this way and that, considering carefully where he had better strike first.

Then how the sparks flew; while he laid on the blows! He turned it, and hammered it, until you could scarcely tell that it had been mended, so skilfully had he joined the parts and beaten them together. Then he filed it smooth, and rubbed it all over with a piece of emery, until it looked as though it were a silver coin just dropped from the mint. When the farmer called, he was a little surprised to hear that the work was done, for he knew John's weakness. But, when he saw the work, and then was asked so reasonable a price for it, he said to himself, as he rode home: "That man has surely got religion. If all of them had it *that way*, I believe I would try it myself."

"Let your light so shine before men, that they may see your good works, and glorify your Father which is in heaven" (Matthew 5:16).

There need be no dubiety about our decisions, when dealing with matters that are positively right or wrong. Frequently, however, difficulty arises in making decision when cases and courses are doubtful. How to die to self in such matters is very aptly illustrated in the following incident, in the experience of the Rev. Evan H. Hopkins, as recorded by Dr. Smellie, his biographer. "Mr. Hopkins wrote, in the summer of 1863, 'I dare say you thought me rather narrow-minded in objecting to accompany the children to the Pavilion Gardens today.' Then he explains the motive which prompted his refusal. 'I feel sure you will agree with me that, as servants of God, we should seek to be guided and led by His hand in all things, and, unless we can look up to Him for His blessing on every step we may be about to take, we may very reasonably question whether we are justified in taking it. Now, I felt that it would be contrary to God's will for me *to be seen* in those gardens; and therefore I could not conscientiously go. At the same time I must not forget that my conscience is not the rule of another man's.' Why was he convinced that God's finger beckoned him away? 'I cannot but think, that if you were fully aware of the injurious influence the Gardens have upon the young, you would feel with me that it is our duty to do all we can to keep them from such enticing scenes. How many could date their ruin from the time they first commenced to attend such places of amusement.'

For Mr. Hopkins the principle in his life was, "Others may, I cannot." The friend to whom Mr. Hopkins wrote had a "broader view," and, summing up, Dr. Smellie says, "It is the difference between the softer and sunnier road of *compromise* and *toleration*, and the uphill track of *separation* and *non-conformity*, and it was characteristic of Evan Hopkins that, by the grace of God, he preferred the uphill track." With what abundantly fruitful results that preference was made, for the glory of God, in the deepening of spiritual life, let Keswick and his world-witness tell.

"Abstain from all appearance of evil"
(I Thessalonians 5:22).

"For the kingdom of God is not meat and drink; but righteousness, and peace, and joy in the Holy Ghost" (Romans 14:17).

A further helpful illustration of how to practice the presence of Christ, and so die to self, is related in a convention talk by the Rev. J.W. Brown. He says, "I had a Sunday School secretary at one time, who was constant in his enmity. He always disagreed. I sat by his side one night, taking a Sunday School Teachers' Monthly Business Meeting, and I had written down on the agenda a certain thing I was going to bring forward, as I thought, for the good of the school.

When we came near to the agenda he looked at me and said, 'Are you going to bring that forward?' 'I thought of doing so.' 'Well, if you do, I shall oppose it.' He always liked to be different. So I said, 'All right, my friend, if that is so we can remedy the difficulty.' I drew my pencil through it. We passed through the items, down to the place where he had a proposal to bring forward for the good of the school; I pressed it and it was passed unanimously. Then he said, 'What about your item?' I said, 'That is off.' He said, 'Won't you bring it forward?' And I said, 'Certainly not, I should not think of doing so.'

Then he urged that I would bring it forward. So I did. And he pushed it through, and it passed unanimously! I am going to make a confession to you. At one time, if that man had opposed my suggestion, I should have wiped the floor with him, and put that thing through wily-nilly. *But the Lord has taught me a better way*, so, by making a concession, I got the victory, and, what is better still, I have his love till this day. I could have made an enemy of him that night. *That is how the message of the Cross works out.*"

(Extract from The Overcomer)

From another sphere of life we cull the following incident. It is the testimony of a student in a Bible training institute with view to service in the foreign field. "I had been used to doing just as I liked, and to having *my own way* in things to a certain degree. The discipline of the College to me at first was irksome. I did not like it at all, and, but for the fact that God had called me, I probably should have left. But I praise God for Whitsun of 1934, when the Holy Spirit dealt with me. From that time onwards there was a radical change in my life. I began to die, and the Lord Jesus began to live."

How to "die daily" may be simplified and summarized in two words:-"*Let Him!*"

"LET HIM!"

Simple words,-yet key to blessing
　　Richer far than speech can tell:
Free to all His name confessing,
　　In whose hearts He thus doth dwell.

For within each true believer
　　Jesus lives,-would live in power,
Longing that He may deliver
　　Each one in temptation's hour.

When within hot words are burning,
    Stinging words,–which rankle sore,
Only "let Him" bear the spurning,
    Thus to find it stings no more.

When your patience ends completely
    With the things that go all wrong,
Only "let Him"–He can sweetly
    Bear with these things, oh, so long.

When your ruffled heart feels fretting
    At the pin-pricks and the stings,
"Let Him" bear these, not forgetting
    He can triumph o'er such things.

When those feelings,–rushed, exciting,
    Rob you of your inward rest,
"Let Him" keep–your look inviting
    Him to reign within your breast.

When that driven sense keeps urging,
    And you almost frantic grow;
"Let Him" meet that inward scourging,
    He can quench the strongest foe.

When the ceaseless tasks keep pressing,
    And you almost would complain,
"Let Him" then meet all depressing
    Sense of burdenedness and pain.

When unhallowed thoughts are filling,
    Aye, and fouling, too, your heart.
Then be simple, yes, and willing
    To "let Him" bid them depart.

When your lonely heart feels breaking
    O'er some cause for deepest grief,
"Let Him" then subdue the aching,
    Let Him in to give relief.

When, if called, to tell the story
    Of the One Who for us died,
Shrink not back,-tell for His glory,
    Just "let Him" the power provide.

When to higher height He leadeth,
    Asking that you yield up all,
"Let Him" meet all your heart needeth
    To respond to such a call.

When His Word speaks, surely, gravely,
   That some things be cleansed away,
Do not fear,—but face all bravely,—
   "Let Him" and His Word have sway.

Key to blessing, rich in measure,
   Key to rest in time of strife,
Key to wondrous inward treasure,
   Key to a triumphant life;—

Not our copy of His goodness,
   Be that copy passing fair,
But just "letting Him" within us
   All things meet and all things bear.
                              (J. Danson Smith)

"If ye know these things, happy are ye if ye do them" (John 13:17).

"Oh, ponder this!" entreats Dr. F.B. Meyer. "The Father wrought perfectly in the yielded nature of Jesus, and the result was summed up in the cry, 'This is my beloved Son in whom I am well pleased.' In some such manner it is possible to walk worthy of God unto all pleasing. It is possible to have this testimony, even in *our* mortal life, that we have pleased God. At the end of every day, as we lie down to sleep, we may hear the whisper of God's voice saying, 'Dear child, I am pleased with you.' But you can only have it by allowing Him, in silence, in solitude, in obedience, to work in you to will and to do of His good pleasure.

Will you begin now? He may be working in you to confess to that fellow-Christian that you were unkind in your speech and act. Work it out! He may be working in you to give up that line of business about which you have been doubtful lately. Give it up! He may be working in you to be sweeter in your home, and gentler in your speech. Begin! He may be working in you to alter your relations with some with whom you have dealings that are not as they should be. Alter them! This very day let God begin to speak, and work, and will; and then work out what He works in. God will not work apart from you, but He wants to work through you. Let Him! Yield to Him, and let this be the day when you shall begin to live in the power of the Mighty Indwelling One."

"Have Thine own way, Lord!
   Have Thine own way!
Hold o'er my being
   Absolute sway!
Fill with Thy Spirit,
   Till all shall see
Christ only, always,
   Living in me."

"Dying with Jesus, by death reckoned mine;
Living with Jesus a new life divine;
Looking to Jesus till glory doth shine
Moment by moment, O Lord, I am Thine.

Never a battle with wrong for the right,
Never a contest that He doth not fight;
Lifting above us His banner so white-
Moment by moment I'm kept in His sight.

Never a trial that He is not there,
Never a burden that He doth not bear,

Never a sorrow that He doth not share
Moment by moment I'm under His care.

Never a heart-ache, and never a groan,
Never a tear-drop, and never a moan,
Never a danger—but there on the throne
Moment by moment He thinks of His own.

Never a weakness that He doth not feel,
Never a sickness that He cannot heal;
Moment by moment, in woe or in weal,
Jesus, my Saviour, abides with me still.

Moment by moment I'm kept in His love,
Moment by moment I've life from above;
Looking to Jesus till glory doth shine;
Moment by moment, 0 Lord, I am Thine."

(D. W. Whittle)

Thirteen-Lessons for each Bible Study Series

The Reading Material

Hardback | 230 Pages | **$12.⁹⁵**

This newest book by Dr. Sexton brings the believer face to face with the responsibility of belonging to a local assembly and actively serving the Saviour through that church. Step by step the reader discovers his personal responsibility to God and the true meaning of church membership. This is the study you have been waiting for to help believers in their understanding of why the Lord Jesus loved the church and gave Himself for it.

The Teacher's Guide Notebook

Three-ring Binder | 98 Pages | **$12.⁹⁵**

The *Teacher's Guide* is a beautifully designed three-ring notebook containing valuable information to assist the teacher in the preparation and presentation of the Bible lesson. Also included are class teaching notes and lesson aims which may be removed from the *Teacher's Guide* and placed in the teacher's Bible to assist in teaching the lesson.

The Study Guide

Paperback | 52 Pages | **$ 2.⁹⁵**

This Study Guide is to be used by each student in the Sunday School class. It contains helpful summaries of each lesson and provides the student with a place to take notes while the lesson is being taught. Questions are also provided to help the student prepare for next week's lesson along with daily Bible readings.

Order All Three for Every Series in the Teacher's Packet
at the reduced price of $21.⁹⁵

The teacher's packet includes all three; the full-length book, the *Teacher's Guide*, and a *Study Guide*.

Order Today!

1-877 AT-CROWN • FAITHfortheFAMILY.COM